YOU CAN'T GET BLOOD OUT OF A TURNIP

Non si può cavar sangue da una rapa

Ilia Terzulli Warner 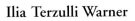 Christopher Arnander

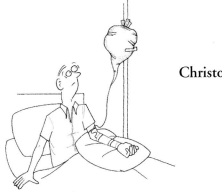

with illustrations by
Kathryn Lamb

STACEY INTERNATIONAL

YOU CAN'T GET BLOOD OUT OF A TURNIP

Stacey International
128 Kensington Church Street
London W8 4BH
Tel: +44(0)20 7221 7166; Fax: +44(0)20 7792 9288
E-mail: marketing@stacey-international.co.uk
www.stacey-international.co.uk

Reprinted 2007

ISBN 1 905299 06 0
2 4 6 8 0 9 7 5 3

British Library Cataloguing-in-Publication Data
A catalogue record for this publication is
available from the British Library

Printed and bound in Singapore by: Tien Wah Press

Preface

I first learned English when I was growing up in Puglia in southern Italy, mostly from popular American songs on rercords which my father and uncle had brought back from Chicago. My favourite numbers were 'Stormy Weather' and 'All I do is dream of you/the whole night through': the latter proved particularly useful because it lists all the seasons and all the months of the year in order. I also began teaching myself out of a primer – this was *Hugo's English for Beginners* – and then, when the British army arrived in 1944, my three sisters and I volunteered to interpret for them. Many years later, when I was tutoring in London, I noticed that my best and brightest A-Level students were still translating word for word. A clever young girl wanted to know if she could render 'It's raining cats and dogs' as '*Piove gatti e cani*'! Sometimes, I myself used to say things such as 'Let dead dogs lie', or 'Anxiety is the spice of life' – and there are many '*finti amici*' that can trip you up. It was this kind of problem that gave me the idea that what people need to learn are idioms, not vocabulary, and that's when I started collecting proverbs.

Choosing a handful of proverbs for this collection has been for me and my collaborator a delightful activity. I'd say that the only headache (*grattacapo*, lit. scratchhead) has been deciding which ones to exclude - there weren't any I wanted to leave out. Nostalgia for my mother tongue was my starting point, as well as the pleasure I've always felt when expressing myself in my adopted language; both have inspired me and made this book easy to put together. I hope that the reader will enjoy *You Can't Get Blood out of a Turnip* as much as I have enjoyed compiling it. Here is another pearl of wisdom (*giudizio*, lit. judgement) to end: '*Il lavoro risana l'anima e il corpo*' ('Work restores body and soul').

Ilia Terzulli Warner
July 2005

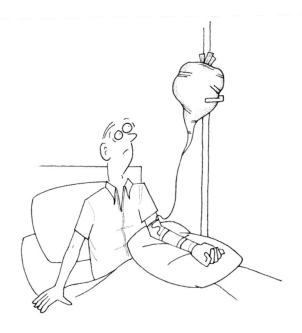

Non si può cavar sangue da una rapa

You can't get blood out of a turnip

You can't get blood out of a stone

Introduction

Lord John Russell's view was that 'a proverb is the wit of one and the wisdom of many', while Lord Chesterfield was dismissive: 'A man of fashion never has recourse to proverbs and vulgar aphorisms.'

Whether fashionable or unfashionable, which of us doesn't use proverbs all the time? They are an indispensable vehicle of popular wisdom and a lively contributor to educated speech. Proverbs are forever evolving this way and that in every language. My co-author, Ilia, and I scratched our heads for an Italian equivalent of 'There's no such thing as a free lunch'. So we invented one: '*Pranzo donato, si paga domani*'.

You Can't Get Blood out of a Turnip is inspired by the success of *The Son of a Duck is a Floater* (1985) and its successors *Apricots Tomorrow* (1991*)* and *Unload Your Own Donkey* (2004). These Arabic/English proverb books, by my wife, Primrose Arnander, and Ashkhain Skipwith, were all three illustrated by Kathryn Lamb; originally compiled in Jeddah, they have brought cross-cultural delight to educated speakers of Arabic and English alike.

The collection is also, in my case, inspired by my mother, Anne Fummi. She lived in Italy for many years and spoke excellent Italian; she greatly enjoyed the study of language and, in particular, proverbs. She and I had compiled a book of Italian and English proverbs, but she died in 1997 before we could complete it.

Our gathering of Italian proverbs is intended to bring to its readers a smile of mutual recognition from the discovery of a pooled aphoristic wit and concision. It won't cut much ice – Italians might say; '*non possono cavare un ragno dal buco*' - among scholars of paremiology. Here is how it goes. Each Italian proverb is given a literal translation and an English equivalent. These are sometimes identical, perhaps because of their common Biblical or Latin origin. Sometimes they are bizarrely askance, as our title illustrates. To the Englishman the turnip is too absurd a vegetable to be borrowed for a metaphor on meanness.

But let us not be over-modest about our book. We are pioneers, in our way, by including among our English renditions certain newly minted sayings which we are betting on becoming tomorrow's proverbs, like *You can't tell a book by its cover* which we will freely equate with *The habit doesn't make the monk*. And, look, here is something of the 21st century for the shared solemnity that you reap what you sow: *Garbage in, garbage out*.

As for our illustrator, Kathryn may not get blood out of a turnip, but she'll get a laugh out of anything she puts her glorious pen to.

Christopher Arnander
July 2005

Prendere due piccioni con una fava

To catch two pigeons with one broad bean

To kill two birds with one stone

Ferisce più la lingua che la spada

The tongue wounds more than the sword

The pen is mightier than the sword

Fra il dire e il fare c'è di mezzo il mare

There's an ocean between saying and doing

Actions speak louder than words

In bocca chiusa non entrano mosche

No flies go into a closed mouth

Silence is golden

Far la vita di Michelaccio

To lead the life of bad old Mick

To lead the life of Riley

Voler andare in paradiso in carrozza

To want to go to heaven in a carriage

To ask for the moon

[To have your cake and eat it]

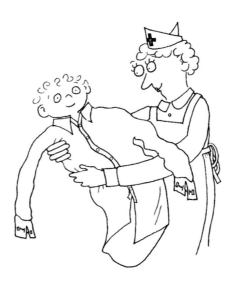

È nato con la camicia

He was born with his shirt on

He was born with a silver spoon in his mouth

Aiutati che Dio ti aiuta

God helps those who help themselves

[*Oliver Cromwell*: 'Praise the Lord and pass the ammunition.']

Le disgrazie sono come le ciliege; una tira l'altra

Misfortunes are like cherries; each brings the other

It never rains but it pours

[*Shakespeare*: 'When sorrows come they come not single spies, but in battalions.']

Il fato manda i biscotti a quelli che non hanno denti

Fate sends biscuits to those who have no teeth

The gods send nuts to those who have no teeth

[An example of Murphy's Law]

Dategli un dito e si prenderà un braccio

Give him a finger and he'll take an arm

Give him an inch and he'll take a mile

Non si sputa nel piatto dove si mangia

Don't spit on the plate from which you eat

Don't bite the hand that feeds you

[Don't cut off your nose to spite your face]

Avere grilli per la testa

To have crickets in the head

To have bats in the belfry

Lavare i panni sporchi in piazza

To wash one's dirty linen in public

Cane non mangia cane

Dog does not eat dog

There is honour among thieves

Nelle sventure si conoscono gli amici

In misfortunes one knows one's friends

A friend in need is a friend indeed

Ognuno ha il suo raggio di sole

Everybody has his ray of sunshine

Every dog has his day

[*Shakepeare*: 'The cat will mew and dog will have his day.']

L'ultima goccia fa traboccare il vaso

The last drop causes the vase to overflow

It is the last straw that breaks the camel's back

Vino dentro, verità fuori

Wine in, truth out

There is truth in wine

[Latin: *In vino veritas*]

Affogarsi in un bicchier d'acqua

To be drowned in a glass of water

To make a storm in a teacup

Non sapere più a che santo votarsi

Not to know which saint to pray to

To be at one's wits' end

Sfondare una porta aperta

To beat down an open door

To push on an open door

O mangi questa minestra o salti dalla finestra

Eat this soup or jump out of the window

Caught between the devil and the deep blue sea

[Beggars can't be choosers]

Tenere il piede in due staffe

To have one's foot in two stirrups

To fall between two stools

[To run with the hare and ride with the hounds]

Non fare il passo più lungo della gamba

Don't take a step longer than your leg

Don't run before you can walk

[Don't bite off more than you can chew]

Non scherzare con l'orso se non vuoi essere morso

Don't play with the bear, if you don't want to be bitten

If you play with fire, you get burnt

Trenta monaci ed un abate non farebbero bere un asino per forza

Thirty monks and one abbot could not force an ass to drink

You can take a horse to water, but can't make him drink

I paperi vogliano portare a bere le oche

The goslings lead the geese to drink

Don't teach your grandmother to suck eggs

La scheggia si ritrae dal ceppo

From the chopping block, the flake is drawn

A chip off the old block

Tale il padre, tale il figlio

Like father like son

Sotto vello di agnello, lupo rapace

Under the lamb's fleece, a rapacious wolf

A wolf in sheep's clothing

Il lupo perde il pelo, ma non il vizio

The wolf may lose his fur, but not his viciousness

The leopard cannot change his spots

Le bugie hanno le gambe corte

Lies have short legs

Your sins will catch up with you

Il bisogno aguzza l'ingegno

Need sharpens talent

Necessity is the mother of invention

[Needs must when the devil drives]

Se non è vero è ben trovato

If it is not true, it's a good invention

[*Note*: the English use the Italian *ben trovato*.]

Ha inventato l'ombrello

He's invented the umbrella

He's reinvented the wheel

Come i topi in campanile

Like mice in a bell-tower

Like a bull in a china shop

La gatta frettolosa fa i gattini ciechi

The hurrying mother cat bears blind kittens

More haste less speed

Quando la gatta non c'è, i sorci ballano

When the cat is not there, the mice dance

When the cat's away, the mice will play

Ad ogni uccello il suo nido è bello

To every bird his nest is beautiful

There is no place like home

[An Englishman's home is his castle]

È il cacio sui maccheroni

It's the cheese on the macaroni

It's the gilt on the gingerbread

Portare acqua al proprio mulino

To bring water to one's own mill

To feather one's own nest

[To look after Number One]

Sui gusti non si disputa

One does not argue about tastes

There's no accounting for tastes

[One man's meat is another man's poison]

Dalla mano alla bocca spesso si perde la zuppa

From the hand to the mouth the soup is often lost

There is many a slip twixt cup and lip

Una mano lava l'altra

One hand washes the other

You scratch my back and I'll scratch yours

[It takes two to tango]

Mangiare per vivere, non vivere per mangiare

Eat to live, not live to eat

Tra i due litiganti il terzo gode

Between two litigants a third benefits

Two dogs strive for a bone, a third runs away with it

Batti il ferro quando è caldo

Hit the iron while it is hot

Strike while the iron is hot

Mentre il cane si gratta, la lepre scappa

While the dog scratches itself, the hare escapes

He who hesitates is lost

Gettare il manico dietro la scure

To throw the handle after the axe

To throw the helve after the hatchet

[To throw the baby out with the bath water]

Preso nelle proprie reti

Caught in one's own nets

Hoisted on one's own petard

[To get a dose of one's own medicine]

Chi ha una testa di vetro non deve gettar pietre ad un altro

If you have a glass head, don't throw stones at others

People who live in glass houses should not throw stones

Non vendere la pelle d'orso prima che sia morto

Don't sell its skin, before the bear is dead

Don't count your chickens before they are hatched

[The opera is not over till the fat lady sings]

La notte porta consiglio

The night brings advice

Sleep on it

Non comprare ad occhi chiusi

Don't buy with closed eyes

Never buy a pig in a poke

Non destare il can che dorme

Don't disturb the sleeping dog

Let sleeping dogs lie

Dalla padella nella brace

From the pan into the embers

Out of the frying pan and into the fire

Acqua passata non macina più

Water that has passed no longer grinds

It's water under the bridge

Chiudere la stalla quando sono fuggiti i buoi

To close the stable door after the oxen have fled

To lock the stable door after the horse has bolted

Goccia a goccia scava la pietra

Constant dropping wears away a stone

[*Shakespeare:* 'Much rain wears the marble.']

Andare a Roma e non vedere il papa

To go to Rome and not see the Pope

To miss the wood for the trees

[Hamlet without the prince]

Svignarsela all'inglese

To slip away like the English

To take French leave

Attacca l'asino dove vuole il padrone

Saddle up the donkey as the master wishes

He who pays the piper calls the tune

Con i soldi si paga e il cavallo trotta

Pay the money and the horse trots

He who pays the piper calls the tune

54

A caval donato, non si guarda in bocca

Don't look a gift horse in the mouth

Chi dorme non piglia pesce

The sleeper doesn't catch the fish

The early bird catches the worm

Una piuma nella mano è meglio di un uccello nell'aria

A feather in the hand is better than a bird in the air

A bird in the hand is worth two in the bush

Del senno di poi sono piene le fosse

From the wisdom of 'afterwards' the ditches are full

It is easy to be wise after the event

Uomo ammogliato uccello in gabbia

A married man is a bird in a cage

Wedlock is a padlock

Voler la botte piena e la moglie ubriaca

To want a full cask and a drunken wife

To get the best of both worlds

Chi trova tiene

He who finds keeps

Finders keepers, losers weepers

Come il cavolo a merenda

Like cabbage at tea-time

To be a fish out of water

[Pork at a Jewish wedding]

Occhio non vede, cuore non duole

What the eye doesn't see, the heart doesn't grieve over

Non c'è fumo senza arrosto

There's no smoke without a roast

There's no smoke without fire

Chi ha fatto 30 può fare 31

Who made 30 can make 31

In for a penny, in for a pound

[*Note*: Pope Leo X appointed 30 cardinals and unexpectedly decided to add one more in 1517]

Chi ha quattrini ha amici

With money one has friends

Nobody knows you when you are down and out

Il diavolo non è brutto come lo si dipinge

The devil is not as bad as he is painted

Give the devil his due

Can che abbaia non morde

The barking dog does not bite

His bark is worse than his bite

L'Inglese italianato

Diavolo incarnato

An Italianate Englishman is the devil incarnate

[*Note*: the proverb derives from English mercenary, Sir John Hawkwood,
who caused havoc in 14th century Italy]

Non è tutto oro quello che luccica

All that glitters is not gold

[*Shakespeare:* 'All that glisters is not gold.']

Agli occhi della madre tutti i figlioli sono belli

To the mother's eyes all her children are beautiful

All her geese are swans

Non è l'abito che fa il monaco

The habit does not make the monk

You can't tell a book by its cover

Il mondo non fu fatto in un giorno

The world was not made in a day

Rome was not built in a day

Tutto il mondo è paese

All the world's a village

It's the same, the world over

[*Marshall McLuhan*: 'The world is a global village.']

Paese che vai, usanza che trovi

Wherever you go, [follow] the customs you find

When in Rome, do as the Romans do

Ridi e il mondo ride con te; piangi e piangerai solo
Laugh and the world laughs with you;
Cry and you cry alone

Lontano dagli occhi lontano dal cuore
Far from the eyes far from the heart
Out of sight out of mind

Anche il verme ha la sua collera

Even a worm can feel indignation

Even a worm will turn

[*Shakespeare:* 'The smallest worm will turn, being trodden on.']

Vecchia gallina fa buon brodo

An old hen makes good soup

There's many a good tune played on an old fiddle

Mandare qualcuno da Erode a Pilato

To send someone from Herod to Pilate

To drive someone from pillar to post

Vecchio innamorato pazzo spacciato

An old man in love is a madman who's done for

There is no fool like an old fool

Gatta inguantata non prese mai topi

A cat in mittens catches no mice

Se non è zuppa è pan bagnato

If it's not soup, it's sodden bread

It's six of one or half a dozen of the other

Molte mani fanno l'opera leggera

Many hands make light work

Troppi cuochi rovinano la minestra

Too many cooks spoil the broth

Il gioco non vale la candela

The game is not worth the candle

The game is not worth the candle

A carnevale ogni scherzo vale

At carnival any prank is acceptable

All is fair in love and war

Bisogna mangiare quel che passa il convento

One must eat what the convent provides

Beggars can't be choosers

[An example of Hobson's Choice]

La superbia andò a cavallo e tornò a piedi

Pride goes on horseback, but returns on foot

The higher you fly the harder you fall

Quel che si semina si raccoglie

What one sows, one reaps

As you sow, so you reap

[Garbage in, garbage out]

Miele non è fatto per gli asini

Honey is not made for asses

Do not cast pearls before swine

[*Shakespeare:* 'Caviar is not for the general' (*i.e.* the generality of people).]

Tizio, Caio e Sempronio

Titus, Caius and Sempronius

Any Tom, Dick or Harry

Per un punto Martin perse la cappa

For the sake of a stitch Martin lost the cloak

To lose the ship for a hap'worth of tar

Portare l'acqua al mulino

To take water to the mill

To carry coals to Newcastle

Chi è sano è più di un Sultano

He who is healthy is more than a sultan

Health is better than wealth

Dimmi con chi vai e ti dirò chi sei

Tell me with whom you are, and I'll tell you who you are

A man is known by the company he keeps

Sbaglia anche il prete a dire la messa

Even the priest stumbles when saying mass

Even Homer nods

Chi sputa in cielo, gli ricade addosso

Who spits at the sky, it falls back on him

Don't piss into the wind

In terra di ciechi, beato chi ha un occhio

In the country of the blind, blessed is the man with one eye

In the country of the blind, the one-eyed man is king

Non c'è peggior sordo di chi non vuol sentire

There's none so deaf as those who will not hear

Cavallo vecchio non cambia andatura

An old horse does not change his gait

You cannot teach an old dog new tricks

Oggi in figura, domani in sepoltura

Today in person, tomorrow in the grave

Here today, gone tomorrow

Pietra mossa non fa muschio

A moving stone makes no moss

A rolling stone gathers no moss

L'ospite e il pesce dopo tre dì rincresce

The guest and the fish are distasteful in three days

After three days fish and guests smell

Avere la mosca al naso

To have a fly in one's nose

To have a bee in one's bonnet

Il medico pietoso fa la piaga cangrenosa

The kindly doctor makes the wound gangrenous

You must be cruel to be kind

Fare di ogni mosca un elefante

To make an elephant from each fly

To make a mountain out of a molehill

[To use a sledgehammer to crack a nut]